DIRECT DEMOCRACY

AMERICANS, TAKE BACK YOUR COUNTRY!

Bo Gunnar Grundberg

M Mosaic Design
Book Publishers

Mosaic Design Book Publishers
Dearborn, MI USA

DIRECT DEMOCRACY:
Americans, Take Back Your Country!
By Bo Gunnar Grundberg
www.NetGet.us

First Printing – March 2015
ISBN: 978-0-9961106-3-1 *(pb)*

Printed in the U.S.A.

0   1   2   3

"O, would some power the gift to give us
to see ourselves as others see us."

Robert Burns
Scottish poet

Preface

Dear Grandpa,

Attached is a report I had to write for my American history class. Our teacher wanted us to present our ideas about what brought about the big change in our country a few years ago. Of course, I was too young then to understand what was going on, but I did a lot of research on the Internet. I hope you like my paper. I'm excited about coming to see you in a couple of weeks!

Love, Karen

How we lost the presidency and congress
and regained our country

Frustrations throughout the American populace bubbled to the top and boiled over when the national debt escalated to $18 trillion with no sign of declining. Apathy had long been another problem; Americans had survived wars, assassinations, and government corruption on many levels, and the ship of state kept sailing. Unbeknownst to them, however, water had been seeping into the ship, dooming it to a remake of the Titanic.

What saved the country from imminent disaster? An astute Internet blog owner spent years ferreting out the truth and exposing government lies on his popular blog, hoping to wake up what he and others called the American sheeple. Over time and with hit-me-where-it-hurts evidence of impending disaster, the people slowly woke up.

An idea was born—an Internet-based system of exercising direct democracy by which the American people would decide the vital issues of the day and thereby take back their country.

They all knew that elected representatives had listened not to their constituents but to the lobbyists who lined their pockets with perks and payoffs. They didn't have to be awake fully to be aware of such shenanigans.

So, you might ask, why did the citizens let their elected representatives get away with that all those years? Well, the population explosion alone made it impossible for Americans to get together in one place and vote on the issues of the day. That worked for small towns and villages in New England but not for a country the size of the United States.

Americans had no choice but to establish a representative government to avoid such a nightmare as we have just described. By electing representatives to vote for a certain number of Americans in each and every state, the system was practical— until the lobbyists came into the picture and took control.

But then, thanks to the Internet, direct democracy was not only a viable alternative to representative government; it was the only way for Americans to take back their country, vote online simultaneously on all issues facing them, and relax, knowing that no special interest groups could thwart their democratic process.

So, one of the DIRECT DEMOCRACY founders asked, "With direct democracy, who needs Congress? And without Congress, who needs a president?"

The DIRECT DEMOCRACY concept, though well-conceived, faced one impediment to its full implementation – the United States Constitution, still revered by the majority of Americans as the Founding Fathers' tried-and-true guide to life, liberty, and the pursuit of happiness.

An amendment to the Constitution was in order, but previously all amendments had been initiated by Congress and then ratified by the states. However, as one sharp student of history pointed out, Article V of the U. S. Constitution provides that two-thirds of state legislatures can petition Congress to call a convention at which amendments could be proposed by the people.

A constitutional amendment requires two-thirds majority vote in both houses of Congress, and then ratification by two-thirds of the states. Once an amendment has been ratified, it becomes the law of the land. Even the Supreme Court can't override it.

How likely would Congress cooperate in passing an amendment to disband itself and, at the same time, make the president a mere figurehead, not unlike European kings and queens?

Something had to be done to keep Congress from burying the amendment in an obscure subcommittee where it would die a slow death.

One of the brains behind DIRECT DEMOCRACY came up with the winning solution—let elected U.S. representatives and senators keep their plush pension, determined on a sliding scale depending on years of service, for a maximum allowance of five years, after which they should be gainfully employed in the private sector. Without lobbyists to fatten their bank accounts any longer, the elected officials decided it was worth the gamble. No work and all that income! They'd be foolish not to accept.

And so, it came to pass one crisp fall day, just before the House and Senate adjourned for cider and doughnuts, these money-grubbing elected officials voted for their own demise by a sizable majority. The president lost all power and instead received the distinction of a goodwill ambassador. With one stipulation: Whoever became president had to be self-sufficient.

No more Air Force One. No more superlative Secret Service staff. (Who would want to kill or kidnap a president who has no power?) No more White House staff and gourmet chefs baking apple-cheddar pie to satisfy bedtime cravings. None of these perks, *unless* the popularly-elected president could support this luxurious lifestyle on his or her own.

After the dust had settled, the American people won back their country. And all it took were busy fingers tapping out truth on keyboards and iPads.

Dear Karen,

What a wonderful report! I'm very proud of your keen interest in the evolution of direct democracy. When you come to Washington, I'll fill you in on some interesting and amazing background stories about Direct Democracy and the national adoption of direct democracy.

By the way, the events happened just as you described them!

I look forward to seeing you soon.

Love,

Grandpa

Introduction

If the American people ever allow private banks to control the issuance of their currencies, first by inflation and then by deflation, the banks and the corporations that will grow up around them will deprive the people of all their prosperity until their children will wake up homeless on the continent their fathers conquered.

Thomas Jefferson
Third United States President

Not so very long ago, two startling new concepts exclusively related to the United States popped up on the Internet. If you were not a regular Internet user, however, these concepts most likely eluded you.

The first concept asserted that the federal income tax (for individuals, not corporations) as dictated by the Sixteenth Amendment to the United States Constitution, initiated in 1913, was *illegal*. In order for a constitutional amendment to become law, it had to have been ratified by three-fourths of the states. At the time, there were only forty-eight (48) states, mandating that no fewer than thirty-six (36) had to ratify any amendment. However, only twenty (20) states ratified the Sixteenth Amendment, thus making it null and void.[1] This meant that ever since this amendment failed to be ratified, millions of Americans had been victimized into paying an illegal individual federal income tax.

This fact had been brought out in numerous court cases that clearly revealed the failure of the federal government to provide clear, undeniable proof that individuals must pay a federal income tax.

The other subject of great interest and intense speculation was how the

Federal Reserve Bank, a privately-owned bank not supervised by the United States Government, had nevertheless managed to finagle a way to set official U.S. financial policy exclusively. The ultimate question was: Who were—and continuously would be—the ultimate benefactors of decisions made by the board of the Federal Reserve: the citizens of the United States or the private owners of the bank?

DIRECT DEMOCRACY is a novel that carefully weaves fact and fiction. If you are a student of American history—past and present—you should have no trouble deciphering the difference between the two. If you are not a history buff but are concerned about why you poured so much money down the federal income tax hole every April 15, you can Google the main topics of this book and learn more about the Federal Reserve and the income tax cases that are cited throughout the book and expanded upon in the End Notes.

The ultimate goal of this book is to encourage Americans to take back their country. The plan that can be used is clearly presented on these pages.

Imagine receiving a letter from the IRS and dreading to open it. Imagine doing so and instead of finding an order for an audit, reading that you no longer have to pay individual federal income taxes.

Stranger things have happened.

Chapter 1

"A majority of the people of the United States have lived
all of their lives under emergency rule. For 40 years, freedoms
and governmental procedures guaranteed by the Constitution have
in varying degrees been abridged by laws brought into force
by statutes of national emergency."

U. S. Senate Report 93-549 (1973)

If you ever have watched a flock of sheep grazing, you know all about the shepherd's hour. Each sheep is perfectly happy to be part of the group, but once a day, each one of them walks up to the shepherd, snuggles, and wants personal attention.

Since I became a grandfather, I have detected the same urge in my grandchildren. Therefore, I was delighted when Karen, nine years old, came to visit me in my townhouse in Springfield, Virginia. Her mother (my daughter) had told her all about Washington, and since Karen was studying government in fourth grade, she was curious to see the big city for herself.

A lot had changed since Karen's mother visited the nation's capital. Most importantly, the United States had been forced into bankruptcy due to a $18 trillion debt because of the disastrous financial policies of the Federal Reserve System.

Karen was curious about what had become of all of the national buildings and monuments. Had they really been auctioned off, like people do with their valuables when they can no longer afford to keep them?

Karen had heard from her teacher that the Capitol Building, once the revered seat of the United States House of Representatives and Senate, had been sold. She wanted to see if it was occupied or empty with a flashing neon VACANCY sign propped up on the front lawn. That was our first stop. To her amazement, she saw a huge, flashing neon sign announcing the opening of the world's largest Chinese culinary center.

Interestingly enough, when the building was auctioned off, the American people retained ownership of one floor, previously occupied by the most influential lobbyists. Now, computers filled the offices on that floor, all programmed to handle the new DIRECT DEMOCRACY system which had been authorized by Congress's last official act.

The DIRECT DEMOCRACY system is an Internet version of direct democracy. Unlike representative democracy, which was practiced in the United States, direct democracy was practiced first in ancient Greece, where all men gathered to vote at the same time in the city square. Since then, many cultures around the world have adopted that same pure form of democracy.

The Vikings, for instance, practiced it. Everyone in each village came together and decided which scenic country to rob next and which slick beauty of a handcrafted ship to show off to the world. To the Vikings' credit, they also introduced a new feature to the direct democracy formula. They allowed women to vote, a rash new feature the ancient Greeks were much too machismo to consider and most certainly not to vote for.

Direct democracy never died. It is still found in enclaves throughout Europe. It is the only form of local government in Appenzell, Switzerland. To decide on their next year's budget and other matters, all male and female citizens (not otherwise disqualified) over the age of twenty must appear personally in the town square on the last Sunday in April. After the traditional debate, each person raises his or her right hand to signify a vote. This has been the supreme legislative authority since 1294.[1]

Karen smiled.

"Our little town in New England still has direct democracy, Grandpa. They hold town meetings. Then everybody there can vote on whatever issues they have been discussing, but they must be present."

"Karen, I'm impressed with your knowledge of the system at work in your town, but, as you noted in your excellent history report, in a country as large as the United States, with the population ever expanding, it became impossible to assemble people in a common place to vote simultaneously. That's when direct democracy was downgraded to a representative system, which has degenerated into a system of bribes, fraud, and graft, ultimately encouraging cash-laden lobbyists to get on board. Influence carries a big price tag.

"Now, thanks to iPads and the Internet, we, like the Vikings, discovered that we could vote simultaneously, do away with the vulnerable representative/lobbyist system, and replace it with pure DIRECT DEMOCRACY on a national level, just as it's now practiced in New England towns like yours."

—◆—

Karen was eager to tell her classmates that she had had lunch in the Capitol, so off we trotted to that huge building. Inside we were faced with a virtual culinary tour of China. There was a splendid array of authentically appointed rooms, each devoted to the cuisine of a specific region of that enormous country: Hunan and Szechwan were popular. There was a huge room just for dim sum, another fashioned like a traditional teahouse with decorative paper lanterns, and even a large gift and food mart for tourists who, upon tasting delectable dishes, could buy the necessary kitchen equipment and food products to make tasty meals at home. Still another restaurant was Chinatown, resplendent in red with a magnificent aquarium and two large murals featuring golden dragons.

But a sleek, contemporary, upscale restaurant with glittering crystal chandeliers, white linen tablecloths, and red phoenix centerpieces, finally caught Karen's eye. Even before we were seated, she insisted on ordering, maybe because I had ordered the last time and that meal hadn't set well with her concept of authentic, gustatory Chinese food.

Karen's order consisted of house specialties such as Congee, Dan Sui Mai, Ma Lai Gao, along with smashed cucumbers in garlic sauce and turnip-filled pastry puffs. I wasn't surprised at her knowledge of Chinese food or her sophisticated taste for exotic cuisine. She had been taking Mandarin lessons in school and was curious about everything in the Chinese culture.

I noticed, however, that every item Karen ordered was the most expensive in its category.

She was her mother's daughter, all right.

After our brief tour of Chinese eating establishments and shops, and our elegant lunch in the Capitol, Karen wondered what else filled the dozens upon dozens of offices in the building. We discovered that almost all of them were filled with Chinese white-collar professionals, diligently working in a wide variety of activities: real estate, oil, gas, and mineral acquisitions, toll-way takeovers, all in the United States, of course.

One small office, occupied by a bespectacled Chinese gentleman, was charged with handling the development of Chinese cities across America. The prototype had been created in a rural area of Michigan, where the Chinese built a city on two hundred acres of farmland for which they paid $1.2 million. The city was not designed to be a tourist trap for Americans to learn about the Chinese lifestyle but for the well-heeled Chinese business people arriving to start companies in the United States.[2]

After a brief tour of the DIRECT DEMOCRACY office, Karen wanted to look at a number of other public office buildings that had changed hands in the U.S. bankruptcy auction. She had discovered that the reason for some of the purchases was almost funny.

So, to give her a good laugh, I drove her past the SEC building. "Some men from the Middle East who had lost fortunes in the Madoff Ponzi scheme bought the building," I told her. "You see, they were upset that although the SEC had been alerted by a stock analyst in Boston of obvious ongoing fraud eight years prior to the day Madoff turned himself in, the SEC had not taken any action. That's why these men lost fortunes. They bought the SEC building with just one diabolic purpose in mind, although they also knew that a profit would ultimately show up.

"They decided to show their displeasure with the SEC by allowing them just three days to clear out their offices. They hired photographers to capture on film the frustrated facial expressions of those imbeciles as they evacuated their files."

"Why didn't they just shred them, Grandpa?"

"There weren't enough shredders in the whole building that could work fast enough on such short notice. The new owners, in relaxed dalliance, took special pleasure, watching as some of the files were dropped, scattering papers down the street with fat, arcane bureaucrats in tight pants frantically running after them."

Karen giggled.

"Grandpa, can we see the IRS building? I wonder what they are doing with it now that people don't have to pay taxes."

"Well, the IRS has retained some offices in the basement. You see, corporate taxes are still legal, so they still have work to do, but they had to cut back on staff and work space. The building itself was bought by an alliance of wealthy, philanthropically-oriented Europeans with a common hatred for repressive, totalitarian regimes. They publicly condemned all countries that had a record of jailing their own citizens for not adhering to illegal, concocted laws invented by authoritarian and often sadistic governments."

"Even movie stars and other famous people have gone to prison for not paying their taxes," Karen said.

"Yes, the United States, directed by the Federal Reserve and its collection arm, the IRS, has jailed countless U.S. citizens since 1913 when what the Fed refers to as the Income Tax Amendment supposedly passed to become the Sixteenth Amendment to the Constitution."

"But, Grandpa, my American history teacher, Mr. O'Brien, told us that it didn't really pass. How can they put people in prison for disobeying a law that isn't really a law?"

I was impressed not only with Karen's eagerness to learn but also with her teacher who is obviously more enlightened than many Americans.

"You see, Karen, there is a fatal flaw. The Constitution requires all amendments to be ratified by a majority of the states in the Union. Only forty-eight states made up the Union in our Lord's year of 1913.

"Records repeatedly, in fact triple-checked, in each state's archives, proved without a shadow of a doubt that only twenty states ratified the amendment, and there are also some pertinent questions as to the legality of the votes even among those twenty states which supposedly passed the amendment.

"So the facts show that a majority of the states did not approve the amendment, thus rendering the Sixteenth Income Tax Amendment null and void."[3]

"Mr. O'Brien showed us a Disney cartoon made during World War II that used Donald Duck and other characters to make people *want* to pay their income taxes," Karen informed me.[4]

"Well, the government, prompted by the Fed, went—and still goes—to great lengths to intimidate people to pay their taxes," I explained. "But the federal income tax for U.S. individuals is non-existent and cannot *legally* be enforced and definitely and most certainly cannot be used to send folks to jail.

"But to answer your question why some people—even those celebrities you mentioned—did go to prison for not paying their taxes, if the case was not decided by a jury, most judges were complicit; that is, because they had to get elected, they were part of the corrupt system of justice in the United States. They were part of the election problem the Americans finally got rid of by instituting DIRECT DEMOCRACY."

"I thought judges were supposed to be fair," Karen said with a furrowed brow on her angelic face.

"Yes, they were supposed to be, but unfortunately they were easily influenced by lobbyists and others who wanted to perpetuate this tax scam.

"The good news is that people finally began to wake up to the startling fact that no U.S. citizen was legally compelled to file a W-4 form or pay a personal income tax. Several organizations, like the Tax Honesty Movement, sprang up to alert the public to this awful scam."

Karen's innocence showed with her next question. "Did the United States go bankrupt because people stopped paying their income tax?"

"Good question. No, that's not what caused our government to go belly-up, but before I explain a bit about what did cause the problem, I should tell you about how personal income taxes really were used.

"The government perpetuated the notion that their taxes went toward the maintenance of our infrastructure, support education, and other services.

Gullible Americans just forked over their hard-earned money in the form of taxes, assuming otherwise they'd be back to driving on dirt roads and sending their kids to one-room schoolhouses.

"The cold, hard reality is that federal income taxes from individuals paid only the interest on the loans of money from the Federal Reserve Bank to the U. S. Treasury Department.[5] Just the interest! Other taxes, such as the state income tax that most people pay, are used to build and repair roads as well as to support education. Considering how both have gone downhill, one wonders where all that money really went."

"Sounds like someone cheated," Karen surmised.

"Now, about the problem that caused the government to go bankrupt: The ill-conceived financial policies of the Federal Reserve ran up the federal $18 trillion debt.[6] I know it's hard to imagine that much money, but there was no way for it to be repaid.

"Just like when an individual gets in over his head, he declares bankruptcy because he cannot possibly repay his debts, the United States had no choice but to go that last-ditch route."

"It must have been brave for some people to refuse to pay taxes, when most of the people obeyed the law, even if it wasn't legal," Karen said. "Do you know about any of those cases, Grandpa?"

"When we get back to my home, I will tell you a little about some of the most successful court cases. The defendants, who refused to pay income taxes, were found innocent and set free by jurors. When you get home, you can find more about them on the Internet.

"Incidentally, all of the defendants who had refused to pay their taxes used the same argument. As a rule, they told the U.S. attorney representing the IRS that they would be happy to pay their taxes. All that the attorney—or the IRS—had to do was to show them the law that said without a doubt that they had to pay a personal income tax."

"So, why didn't the attorney show them the law?" Karen queried.

"He couldn't, because there was no such law! Think of it, Karen. If there had been a law, wouldn't it have been much easier—and much less a waste of court time—for any attorney representing the IRS to produce the paper that proved the law exists? It would have been an open-and-shut case. In fact, most of these cases, if not all of them, would never have ended up in court, because the defendants said they would have paid the tax if the IRS had shown them the law that required them to do so."

"This seems to prove that there is no law, which is exactly the opposite of what they are trying to tell the people," Karen said with a certain mystified look on her face.

"It is really quite amusing, Karen, and I hope you will read the court records to see how the IRS lawyers continuously got lost in their own labyrinths, trying to explain the total absence of that darn law.

"So, back to our tour," said Karen. "Who bought the IRS building, and what is it being used for now?"

"An international charity, funded by a few culturally prominent people who despise the illegal imprisonment of anyone in a civilized country, bought the building and turned it into a museum honoring all U.S. citizens who were illegally, even brutally imprisoned or threatened by the IRS for failing to obey this phantom law. The walls of this building are now covered in plaques honoring these fake unfortunate felons."

"The families and descendants of these illegally harassed and imprisoned Americans will therefore be urged to apply for assistance, should there be a financial hardship."

"That's great, Grandpa! Does anyone still pay a federal income tax?"

"Well, yes and no. Individuals no longer pay them, but corporations pay taxes. However, the total corporate tax paid annually exactly matched the country's national defense expenditures. It's another reason why individuals never needed to pay taxes. Anyway, since the United States went bankrupt, wiping out that $18 trillion debt, perhaps no one should pay taxes anymore.

"Karen, here is another thought. I would love to find out just where the $2.6 trillion went.[7] The U.S. Treasury over the years borrowed from the money we all have deposited in our Social Security Trust Fund. That borrowing of our personal money was done under the specific direction of the Federal Reserve Bank."

"It seems like no one watched what the Federal Reserve Bank did. Wasn't there any oversight?"

Again, I was amazed at her depth of knowledge, but kids these days learn a lot, not only in school but on the Internet.

"Karen, there was no transparency or oversight, as you said, and that was the big problem. In fact, the families who owned this bank never allowed an audit; furthermore, they tried to prevent the United States from operating its government through the Internet because it rendered their privately-owned Federal Reserve Bank transparent.

"By the way, here is an example in the public record of the Federal Reserve Bank's sense of privacy and outrageous independence.

"When Senator Bernie Sanders of Vermont awhile back publicly asked former Federal Reserve Bank Chairman Bernanke to show the list of institutions given $2.2 trillion of taxpayers' money deposited in the Federal Reserve Bank by the U.S. Treasury, a calmly arrogant Bernanke, always didactic in upbraiding the government, felt sufficiently secure in his power and simply refused to answer the question.[8]

"As a matter of fact, the curious situation is that the U.S. government had no law that gives it jurisdiction over the privately-owned Federal Reserve.

"We'll talk more about this later. Let's head home."

On our way, we drove by the White House, which had been auctioned off but was not open for tourists. According to rumor, it was snapped up by a descendant of a European banker who had originally provided some of the capital for the incorporation of the Federal Reserve on Jekyll Island.[5] He had purchased it as a Morning Gift for his new wife. This extraordinary gift, an age-old tradition in his family, was given to the new bride on the couple's first morning as husband and wife. He did convert part of the White House to a national museum and rented out living quarters and office space for the powerless president and his or her family.

"My sister, Holly, visited the Statue of Liberty to see what the new owners were doing with it. She said that they spoke with heavy Asian accents and charged excessive fees, like people do when they try to sell their tickets to sports games at higher prices."

"I think they call that scalping, Karen," I said.

"Yes, that's it. Well, anyway, one of the owners came up behind Holly and pinched her butt. He was so sneaky about that, she couldn't tell which of the owners actually did it."

"Well, you have to admit Holly has a cute behind."

"By the way, what's this about Georgia having a new neighbor to the south?" Karen asked.

"Well, that $2.6 trillion taken from the Social Security fund at the advice of the Federal Reserve was a staggering amount. That was the subject of a national debate to decide how it should be rectified.

"Technically the U.S. bankruptcy wiped out all debts. The complication was that since those trillions were taken at the advice of the Federal Reserve, where did the money end up? With the private owners of the Federal Reserve? Then how could we steal from ourselves? Besides, only the Social Security beneficiaries were the victims, not the entire population. In order to reimburse these folks, funds had to be raised by selling a few states belonging to us all. Florida and Hawaii were mentioned because of their splendid climate.

"China had made an offer to help Cuba take over Florida, but when the Georgians discovered that they might have to share their southern border with Cuba instead of Florida, the news did not receive a positive resonance. All hell broke loose. One thing the folks in Georgia can do better than the rest of us is talk, and that idea was quickly put aside."

"Maybe those Chinese were the same ones we saw working in the real estate office at the Capitol," Karen said.

Chapter 2

"The few who understand the system, will either be
so interested in its profits, or so dependent on its favors that
there will be no opposition from that class, while on the other hand,
the great body of people, mentally incapable of comprehending
the tremendous advantages...will bear its burden without complaint,
and perhaps without suspecting that the system is inimical
to their best interests."

Rothschild Brothers of London
Communiqué to associates in New York
June 25, 1863

By the time we arrived at the house, Karen was bursting with questions. What an inquisitive girl! I think she gets this from me.

"First of all, Grandpa, how did the United States get into this terrible mess in the first place, and second, in the early days of DIRECT DEMOCRACY, why did you think it would work here?"

"To answer your first question, I have to go all the way back to 1913, when some of the world's most powerful financial people, who privately owned the Federal Reserve Bank, had somehow managed secretly to take over the direction of all U. S. economic policies.

"However, even with the horrible results of the Fed's catastrophic policy running up that $18 trillion debt, there was fortunately some hilarious comedy associated with the creation of the Federal Reserve."

"Where did it start?" Karen asked.

"This disastrous private bank was not, as generally believed, created in a smoke-filled room in Washington but on Jekyll Island, Georgia, an island privately owned by some of the world's wealthiest banking families.[1]

"At the time when these bankers traveled by private railroad cars to meet and organize the bank, they were repeatedly told to use only their first names when addressing each other. The servants were kept in the dark, as the world's most important men were obviously up to something absolutely no good.

"In view of the huge U.S. deficit and the mega inflation that happened as a result of their financial misguidance, it's no wonder they were desperate to remain anonymous.

"Their devilish reason for setting up the private Federal Reserve Bank and getting its privacy approved by Congress was to allow them to run the entire U.S. economy."

"Did anyone ever find out who these financial giants were?" Karen asked.

"Yes, a number of people probed long enough and finally learned the identity of the founders of the Federal Reserve. The cartel was comprised of the following:
— Rothschild Banks of London and Berlin
— Lazard Brothers Banks of Paris
— Israel Moses Seif Banks of Italy
— Warburg Bank of Hamburg and Amsterdam
— Lehman Brothers of New York
— Shearson American Express
    (formerly Kuhn, Loeb Bank of New York)
— Goldman Sachs of New York
— National Bank of Commerce, New York,
    Morgan Guaranty Trust [2]

"Here's a startling fact: the Federal Reserve was the only for-profit corporation in America that was exempt from both federal and state taxes. The Fed took in about $1 trillion per year tax-free! The banking families I just listed got all that money."[3]

"What!"

"You heard correctly, but it bears repeating because it is so shocking. *The*

Federal Reserve was the only for-profit corporation in America that was exempt from both federal and state taxes. The Fed takes in about $1 trillion per year tax-free!"

"That doesn't seem fair, Grandpa," said Karen, shaking her head.

"The Board of Governors awhile back was interesting too:

— Ben Shalom Bernanke, chairman, Board of
    Governors of the Federal Reserve until 2020

— Donald L. Kohn, vice-chairman, Board of Governors
    until 2016

— Randall S. Kroszner, member, Board of Governors

— Frederic S. Mishkin, member, Board of Governors

— Alan Greenspan, advisor and former chairman.[4]

"By the way the Fed's top people were all painfully aware of the bank's questionable origin and foreign, private ownership. It was therefore a hilarious comedy watching how they publicly put up a veneer of omniscient authority, a studied display of conspicuous tranquility, an attitude of studied indifference. Yet they were all instantly ready to wet their pants as the bank some day would run into another John Kennedy, too nimble to get shot, who would finally unmask them."

"Incidentally, you would never have seen the above paragraph quoted in the mainstream media, only on YouTube, one of our very few bastions of free press promised by our Constitution. When the Feds were unmasked, the media barons' pants got even wetter since they were fully aware that in their role as the nation's conscience, they should have pounced on the Fed's defrauding of America. Some day, surprisingly soon, their licenses to publish will be up for bids."

"Good! The media should always tell us the truth or at least make a real effort to learn the truth," Karen noted.

"Back to the origins: G. Edward Griffin got to the bottom of the shenanigans on Jekyll Island. He wrote a book about it, called *The Creature from Jekyll Island.* [5]

"It was definitely titillating to learn that Paul Warburg, European-born scion of that still immensely powerful European banking family, was the author of the Federal Reserve Act, which stripped the United States of all its economical rights and gave all future U.S. financial policies to the fiscal tyranny of a small group of private bankers.[6]

"One of the founders of the Federal Reserve, Mayer Amschel Bauer Rothschild, made a brazen statement: 'Let me issue and control a Nation's money and I care not who makes its laws.'[7]

"Setting up the Federal Reserve Board, in time, turned out to be immensely profitable for this small group of bankers, but for the United States, it was the beginning of a catastrophic inflation that ballooned from that time on."

"It sounds like these guys had been planning this for a long time, Grandpa."

"Yes. Before the Jekyll Island meeting, the bankers had their system worked out in detail, a winning formula that permitted them to lend $9,000 for each $1,000 that the public deposited in their banks.

"This formula was recently confirmed and revealed by the appointed receiver in the Lehman Brothers' bankruptcy case. He examined the Lehman books and compared the capital on deposit with the amount of the outstanding loans. The receiver's astounding figures are available on the Internet.[8]

"It seems they weren't very good at covering up this formula, were they?"

"No, they weren't. The real reason for the Jekyll Island meeting and the organization of this private Federal Reserve Bank was their desperate need, first, to get their hands on the U.S. printing presses to create their phantom paper dollars, and even more important, to set U.S. financial policy, an implicit guaranty to do their printing privately without supervision or audit.

"Now comes something really funny.

"Pure comedy.

"Some of the dollars they were allowed to print on U.S. printing presses they then lent back to the United States and charged interest!

"Legally."

"That took a lot of nerve," Karen said.

"Yes, it did. Incidentally and incredibly, this had been going on since

1913, until we changed to the DIRECT DEMOCRACY system.

"This was something Congress did not understand when they ceded to a private corporation the right to set U.S. economic policy.

"From that day forward, whenever a decision had to be made and actions taken, whose profit and welfare do you think would have topped the list? It was always the client—in this case, the United States or the private owners of the Federal Reserve—some of the world's greediest people."

"They had this all planned out, didn't they?" asked Karen.

"Indeed. Look, here are three indisputable and totally devastating facts, the direct results of the Fed's disastrous (for us) financial policy.

"First, under the Fed's leadership, an item costing $1 in 1913, you had to pay $22.55 for it in 2012.[9] This is easily a sign of runaway inflation. Throughout history, inflation has been the prime cause of financial catastrophes and collapse of countless national economies.

"The second reason for the U.S. bankruptcy was that under the privately owned Federal Reserve Bank's greedy direction, the U.S. economy acquired a $16 trillion debt, and an additional request to increase the official limit to $19 trillion.

"The third reason, which finally brought the crisis to a head, was the fact that all personal income taxes collected by IRS—the Federal Reserve's collection arm—since 1913 had been collected fraudulently under false pretenses using a non-existent phantom law and must therefore be legally refunded.

"Absolutely nobody was surprised therefore when the United States found itself in need to declare bankruptcy.

"Nobody could understand why the United States, as a matter of fact the only country in the entire history of the world, allowed its economic policy to be directed by a private corporation exclusively owned by wealthy individuals, all now super wealthy."

From the expression on Karen's face, she obviously was amazed at all that I had told her.

"Okay, so through DIRECT DEMOCRACY, the American people finally got rid of the Federal Reserve. What did they replace it with, Grandpa?"

"That is an easy question, Karen. If you get rid of cancer, what do you replace it with? We would restore the power to the U.S. Treasury that it once had.

"Now take a look at the U.S. financial collapse of 2008. Who did the Federal Reserve give billions after billions to? The banks.

"In 2012, Senator Bernie Sanders of Vermont exposed the names of eighteen current and former Federal Reserve regional bank directors. The banks and businesses of these directors received more than $4 trillion in near-zero-interest Federal Reserve loans after the 2008 fiscal collapse.

"One of the directors was Jamie Dimon, CEO of the largest bank, JP Morgan Chase, who served on the Federal Reserve Board of New York since 2007. His bank received $390 billion of the $4 trillion total! On June 12, 2012, he testified before a Senate committee investigating how his bank recently managed to lose at least $2 billion in risky investments, involving some of the same questionable practices that brought the 2008 collapse.

"These banks gave bonuses to their CEOs while, at the same time, millions of Americans were losing their homes to the very same banks. If the Federal Reserve really had the welfare of Americans in mind, shouldn't they have helped these Americans rather than the bankers?"

"Why did it take so long for people to figure out how these greedy people were manipulating the American people?" Karen inquired.

"In reality, a great American spoke out against the idea of central banking even before the Federal Reserve came into being."

"Who was that?" Karen asked.

"Abraham Lincoln. He tried his best to prevent the Rothschilds from interfering in the Civil War with their financial finagling. The Rothschilds won, but afterward, President Lincoln issued a warning to the American people:

"'The money power preys upon the nation in time of peace and conspires against it in times of adversity. It is more despotic than monarchy, more insolent than autocracy, more selfish than bureaucracy. I see in the near future a crisis approaching that unnerves me, and causes me to tremble for the safety of our country. Corporations have been enthroned, an era of corruption will follow, and the money power of the country will endeavor to prolong its reign by working upon the prejudices of the people, until the wealth is aggregated in a few hands, and the republic is destroyed.'[10]

"Maybe he was assassinated because of this warning," Karen suggested.

"The coincidence of death surrounding public figures who have opposed central banking, in general, and the Fed, specifically, started even before Lincoln who died in 1865. President Andrew Jackson vetoed the charter for the Bank of the United States on July 10, 1832. There was an unsuccessful assassination attempt on his life, after which he remarked to his vice president, 'The bank, Mr. Van Buren, is trying to kill me...'[11]

"Then, after Lincoln, came James Garfield, the twentieth U.S. president and former chairman of the House Appropriations Committee. He didn't mince words either about central banking, stating that whoever controls the currency supply would control the business and activities of all people. Four months after his inauguration, Garfield was shot to death at a railroad station on July 2, 1881.

"Garfield had this to say about central banking:

'Whoever controls the volume of money in our country is absolute master of all industry and commerce...and when you realize that the entire system is very easily controlled, one way or another, by a few powerful men at the top, you will not have to be told how periods of inflation and depression originate.'[12]

"Grandpa, this is starting to sound scary."

"Okay, we'll take a break from assassinations for a bit. In 1916, people protested against the Federal Reserve Bank. One such person was President Woodrow Wilson himself, under whose watch the 1913 Christmas Day *coup d'etat* created the Federal Reserve Bank while most of Congress was home drinking spiked eggnog. Wilson declared that the takeover of the duties of the U.S. Treasury by a privately owned bank was a disaster."[13]

"'I am a most unhappy man,' said Wilson. 'I have unwillingly ruined my country. We have come to be one of the worst ruled, most completely controlled and dominated governments in the civilized world, no longer a government by free opinion, no longer a government by conviction and the vote of the majority, but by the opinion and duress of a small group of dominant men.'[14]

"Perhaps here would be a good place to quote former President George H. W. Bush, "If the American people really knew what we had done, we would be chased down and lynched."[15]

Suddenly Karen's face lit up.

"Wait! We can't forget President Kennedy. Mr. O'Brien, who is a big Kennedy fan, told us that Kennedy tried to get rid of the Federal Reserve Bank on June 4, 1963 when he issued Executive Order No. 11110.[16] Kennedy was shot just a few months later. I wonder if there was any connection between his executive orders and his assassination."

"How did you remember that date and the executive order number?" I asked, amazed that those facts would stick in her young, active mind.

"Mr. O'Brien said that those facts are important ones to remember, so I just did.

"Anyway, Mr. O'Brien also told us that those executive orders never have been reversed, amended or replaced. According to the Constitution, any of the presidents after Kennedy could have carried them out.

"Well, if any president after Kennedy tried, I wonder if they would have been assassinated too," Karen wondered aloud. "Maybe they were all too afraid."

"I do have to give Reagan credit for at least one good quote," I interjected, "He said, 'I believe that in both spirit and substance, our tax system has come to be un-American.'"

Karen took a moment to finish her ice cream.

"I was thinking about something Mr. O'Brien has us do for fun," said Karen, as a broad smile deepened her dimples. "It's sort of a vocabulary test."

"What does a vocabulary test have to do with the subject we're talking about?" I quizzed.

"Well, he said that since all of the presidents since President Kennedy have disappointed us by not carrying out Kennedy's Executive Order, we should give them descriptive titles."

"You know, the Europeans always added an adjective to each of their kings' names," I said, "but usually they did that long after they were dead and gone. Names like Richard the Lionhearted and Peter the Great."

"Mr. O'Brien challenged us. The student who came up with the best descriptive title could go to the faculty room where he would help with the next day's assignment."

"So, what names did you and your classmates come up with?" I asked.

"Lyndon Johnson, The Chicken-hearted

"Richard Nixon, The Lily-livered

"Gerald Ford, The Gutless

"Jimmy Carter, The Benign

"Ronald Reagan, The Pusillanimous

"George H.W. Bush, The Coward

"Bill Clinton, The Dodger

"George W. Bush, The Spineless

"Barack Obama, The Clown

"I won with 'The Pusillanimous'," Karen proudly proclaimed. "I had originally picked "The Pussy," but I liked Ronald Reagan in his old cowboy movies, so I made his name sound a bit more dignified."

I had a good laugh. "You mean you watched Reagan in those old flicks?"

"Yes," she said, "I think Mom had a crush on him, and she likes to watch the old movie channels. Sometimes his old films pop up, and I watch them with her."

Karen continued, "So, after our vocabulary tests, Mr. O'Brien always commented: 'An obviously sorry bunch when compared with JFK and the other true heroes in our history.'"

"Your teacher is right," I said, "The Feds were in full charge of our economy and ran up this huge debt, which made them low-hanging fruits, but none of our brave presidents, obviously worried about getting killed had so far helped Kennedy to eliminate the Federal Reserve."

It sure is fun having grandchildren as bright as Karen. She then mentioned something Mr. O'Brien had told them.

First, she opened her purse.

"Here is the five dollar bill you gave me when you picked me up at the airport. By the way, my grandfather up in Stowe always gives me a twenty dollar bill, but Mother said not to mention it since we all know how careful you are with money."

I was flattered.

She had used the word "careful." I had expected "cheap," but this was too much fun to pass up.

"So, you are giving me back my fiver?"

Karen laughed. "Not a chance. I just want you to see something Mr. O'Brien showed us."

She held up the five dollar bill. "Look at the top of the note. What do you see?"

"Federal Reserve Note," I said.

"Mr. O'Brien said that the secretive owners of the Federal Reserve Bank had issued this five dollar paper note, backing the value with what?"

"Nothing!"

"Right! As Mr. O'Brien said, 'Not even a whiff of hot air!'"

"Then he showed the class a ten dollar bill that his grandfather had given to him. There was a different message on that bill."

"Yes, Karen, and when President Kennedy issued his executive order, he made the Federal Reserve stop printing money and give that power back to the U. S. Treasury."

"Right, and on all those bills, Kennedy had the Treasury print: Silver Certificate. This certifies that there is on deposit in the U. S. Treasury in silver payable to the bearer on demand. Clearly spelled out."

I then explained to Karen, "When the Federal Reserve crowd took over the U.S. Treasury in 1913, we had gold in *them there* Fort Knox hills. Kennedy discovered fifty years later that we had no gold, just silver.

"As soon as Kennedy was assassinated, the Federal Reserve Bank quickly diverted the Kennedy silver notes out of circulation and substituted their own bits of paper."

"What about the silver that President Kennedy found? Where is it now?" Karen asked.

It seems, I am not the only curious one.

"You have heard about Ron Paul, who ran for president in 2008 and again in 2012. He demanded that the gold and silver in Fort Knox be audited.[17]

"So far, no audit has been forthcoming.

"By anyone.

"But, on another front, after working three years to garner support, Congressman Ron Paul finally succeeded in getting HR459, his Federal Reserve Transparency Act bill out of the House Oversight Committee. If passed into law, the Government Accounting Office (GAO) would be required to do a top-to-bottom audit of the Fed's board of governors and 12 regional banks. It would also require the Fed to reveal its private monetary policy deliberations. As in who received $27 trillion in bail-out funds since 2008.[18]

"Incidentally, about 3 percent of the Kennedy silver notes are still out there somewhere."

After dinner that night, I handed Karen my laptop.

"Karen, let's have some fun.

"We have all heard how our mainstream media empires declare their frenzied support for free speech, a *sacred* American right to be honored, even to die for if necessary.

"Here take my lap top."

Karen opened up to the Internet.

"Now, go to the browser's search box and type in www.shreveporttime. com, the website for the local Louisiana paper by the same name.

"Now ask what you can find out about Thomas W. K. Cryer, court case #5.06-cr50164-SMH-MLH-ALL, and his successful jury trial about his refusal to pay his U.S. federal income tax, claiming that there is no such law compelling him to do so."[19]

Karen spent a few seconds scrolling through the list.

"Here it is.

"Read it, and you will discover that the jury found that there is no law authorizing the federal government to collect an individual income tax from any U.S. citizen.

"Now, Karen, if you find this hard to believe, you can check this out for yourself. First, read the Constitution, which clearly states that any amendment in order to be legal must be ratified by a majority of the states. Here, use my little pocket edition of the Constitution."

Karen took a few minutes to search for the correct part of the Constitution and read it carefully.

"You're right, Grandpa. It says it right here in Article V. That's the same article I mentioned in my history report."

"Yes, you're right. Now, go to every state capital and then to their Secretary of the State's office to find out when the Sixteenth Amendment—the income tax amendment—was ratified. You will discover that only twenty of the forty-eight states ratified that amendment. (See chart in End Notes.)

"Now type in Cryer and his court case again and see what you can find about the coverage of the CBS, NBC, ABC, and the *New York Times* of this truly historical and successful court case."

Karen diligently searched all the major news media websites.

"What did you find?"

"Nothing, Grandpa. Why?"

"The media barons have sold out their role as the country's conscience.

"The media billionaires are fully aware that if the American public learned that the law compelling them to pay individual income taxes is non-existent, the ramifications could be catastrophic for them. After all, the media's implied duty is to keep the public informed.

"They are fully aware that as co-conspirators in withholding the truth, their individual broadcasting and publishing licenses would be cancelled eventually.

"Since they are in bed together, there is no discernable daylight between the media moguls and the Federal Reserve's anonymous owners, and since they constantly intermingle in the same rarified financial stratosphere, the subject of intentionally misleading the American public comes up.

"However, they are aware that if Americans stopped paying the illegally concocted federal income tax, this unique form of self-invented official tyranny on the part of these moguls would collapse.

"Their velvet-cushioned world would disintegrate because their standard of living was sustainable only through the criminal windfall from this fraudulent income tax paid by the grossly misled American population."

"Newspapers are unable, seemingly, to discriminate between a bicycle accident and the collapse of civilization."

George Bernard Shaw
Irish playwright & critic
1856-1950

"Grandpa, when was the income tax created?"

"Well, if you guess right, I'll give you another fiver."

"I guess you can keep it, Grandpa. I haven't got a clue."

"It was created the same year—1913—as the Federal Reserve.[20] That was no coincidence. If the Fed was going to create debt, it had to create some way to have it repaid."

"That sounds like a magic trick, Grandpa."

"Well, magic is all about illusion, isn't it? If you create an illusion that you have lent real money to someone, you have to create a real *someone* to repay you. That's exactly what happened with the Fed and the IRS."

The next morning, I took Karen to the airport for her return to New England.

As I handed her over to a waiting stewardess in front of security at Reagan International Airport, I gave Karen a twenty dollar bill.

As I handed her that piece of paper privately printed by the Federal Reserve, after saying thank you, Karen smiled and added: "Peer pressure."

I was laughing as I drove off.

That nine year old is bright.

—◈—

Karen really got me thinking about the Fed and all the damage it's done to the U. S. economy. I decided to explore the issue further. I also put Lucia, my favorite researcher, to help me dig up more evidence, and she really came up with some great material.

Chapter 3

Democracy…while it lasts is more bloody than
either aristocracy or monarchy.

John Adams
Second United States President

Since folks through DIRECT DEMOCRACY would make all the decisions,
why would we need a president?

After all, our presidency is a relic, a direct descendant of those decadent
European royal regimes; our presidential administrative bureaucracy has
assumed the role of the antiquated royal court and its favored advisors.

When the constitution was written in 1787, there were no less than thirty-
two kings and emperors around the world, seventeen just in Europe, all with
absolute executive power, fiercely fighting each other with constant wars.

In an attempt to raise our presidency to an equal powerful royal status,
the writers of the constitution felt motivated to give our president equal royal
executive power, and have we suffered ever since.

Fortunately, the world has gradually discovered the lunacy in letting one
individual decide the fate of a country, and practical folks began to kill, expel,
and imprison their kings, although a few royals have been kept, albeit totally
emasculated just as historical show pieces.

Now consider the consequences of eliminating the office of presidency.

There would be no more $1.4 billion annual presidential budget and,
above all, no more presidential wars.

In the future, we would go to war only if a majority of us believed it would be the right thing to do. Many of the past presidential wars have been judged redundant.

With direct vote, our soldiers would die only in a country they judged worth saving, hopefully very few.

One of our problems with powerful presidents is that lately our culture has not produced folks with the same quality in principles and goals as those of our Founding Fathers.

Another handicap with our presidency is the fact that often in the past, we have picked presidents from our politicians, people often proven to be the most repellent, tawdry, pathetic outcast of misfits this earth have ever seen.

They often had no financial or any other organizational successes to show except brilliantly arranging for the lobbyists to bribe them.

Keep in mind the crown jewel of DIRECT DEMOCRACY is that it gives the executive power back to the people.

Maybe due to old-fashioned sentiment, we might still decide to keep the presidential image alive and open.

Then we would elect someone to represent the country but without executive power; just a figurehead like the present puppet kings in Europe.

Under our new DIRECT DEMOCRACY, we could thus impress the world with some genuinely intelligent presidents who have already proved their brilliance by what they have personally accomplished.

But those new presidential candidates would have to have oodles of money. Why not make them personally responsible for the entire presidential budget and, on top, charge them astronomical rents to live in our beloved White House? They will get the glory; let them pay for it.

Besides, wouldn't it be fun to watch those billionaires have a ball, spending their own money rather than ours, making their presidency glamorous?

And we would have the media follow them around, observing how intensive inventive they can be, offering new ideas on how to be a self-made U.S. president by throwing their own billions around in a spectacular way.

This would naturally inspire youngsters to grow up, be successful, make a lot of money, and become presidents too.

It is assumed, by popular demand, the first candidate who wins must give the White House rose garden a brand new look. The present rose garden has the squalor and air of a nasty nest of lies.

The only billionaire candidates to be allowed to run for the presidency of United States would be the ones who had accumulated their wealth through their own efforts.

They would most likely come from entrepreneurs, inventors, or geniuses from the computer world.

The ones with the most modest background would be instant favorites. Anybody with an inherited fortune would not be allowed to run.

The presidency would then become an internationally envied example of what this country stands for and what can happen here if you are stubborn about working hard and are creative.

These new presidents would be living proof that our American culture can produce intellectual giants.

We will be offering them a stage on which to parade their brilliance and fortune.

A suggested new title: His Billionaire Internet Excellency, our first DIRECT DEMOCRACY-elected president.

There would still be some spectacular competition among these dynamos to get elected because of their individual Humana qualities.

And we would look them over and decide on the most attractive. After all, they would represent all of us, and we Americans sure are a good-looking breed.

He would be a new kind of president, a dynamic success, a financial miracle maker, now ready to spend his own funds, celebrating his deserved reward, namely receiving the ultimate honor of getting elected president of the United States.

In time, we will all be able to hear the envy as the world applauds.

Since our inherited conception of the necessity of the presidency is so inbred, it will take a major exercise in logic and reasoning to cure our inherited lunacy in allowing a single individual to decide our future.

Chapter 4

Never doubt that a small group of
thoughtful, committed citizens can change the world;
Indeed, it's the only thing that ever has.

Margaret Meade

To convince the stalwart lunatics among us who are convinced that the presidency is an untouchable, sacred institution we have some wonderful and startling news.

By doing away with our unmanageable colossus of a government, and substitute our sleek DIRECT DEMOCRACY we can make our country a private, financially self-sustained entity.

Voter/Marketing is a brand new multi-trillion-dollar marketing concept.

Under DIRECT DEMOCRACY, every registered voter will be a decision-making entity in a two-way communication network, which will stay in constant touch with more consumers than Google, Facebook, YouTube, and Amazon combined.

As you consider the astronomical commercial implication presented by this new network, suddenly Boston University's Dr. Kotlikoff's $222 trillion U.S. debt incredibly becomes manageable.

DIRECT DEMOCRACY is a miraculous self supporting re-invention, an unexpected gift from the ancient Greeks.

To the hard-to-convince, please note that the concept of our government being engaged in private business is not as revolutionary as you might think.

The U.S. Post Office has already initiated a policy proven prolific, profitable for that cash-strapped department by offering to send out advertisements paid for by independent corporations, which are included in a welcome package every one of us receive when we change our address.

Can you imagine the billions of dollars that private companies will pay for the opportunity of introducing their products through a semi-government network of implied integrity and value, examined, tested and approved by none less than Uncle Sam?

To call it staggering is not a stretch.

Besides, there is that other festering concept intentionally hidden and untouchable because of the expected pain.

A country that has fought communism for generations, if not centuries, simply cannot *allow* itself to go bankrupt partly at the hands of a communistic nation.

How could we possible explain to history how our open, freedom-loving nation went bankrupt because of money we borrowed and could not pay back to that corrupt, despised communistic world?

Only a few of us are aware that $1.3 trillion of our debt is owed to China.

Still, of equal interest, $2.6 trillion is owed to our Social Security and $2.1 trillion to private, mostly foreign, bankers who are the sole owners of the Federal Reserve Bank, supposedly our own national bank but engaged in a secretive fleecing of our country to the benefit of the Federal Reserve Bank's private mostly foreign owners.

Most of the remaining balance of Dr. Kotlikoff's trillions U.S. debt is owed in the form of unfunded commitments such as pensions, grants, and other benevolent legislative excesses.

Finally, we have a way out, a method to pay our U.S. debt and do away with this monstrous organization that has placed us in our financial hell hole: NetGet.

Chapter 5

Remember, democracy never lasts long.
It soon wastes, exhausts, and murders itself.
There is never a democracy that did not commit suicide.

John Adams
Second United States President

The question is, of course, what would it take to shame and bribe our country's crooked professional politicians into voting to disband them?

How do we convince them that the Internet has eliminated the need for their shameful profession, entitlements, and free ride?

What this constitutional convention really intends to do is take the vote and power away from the lobbyists and give it back to the people.

Since the lobbyists have managed to make the discipline of buying votes pervasive, the only unknown is the amount of cash they pay the politicians for them.

The question therefore facing us now is how much cash would it take for our politicians to agree to financial suicide?

We would have to offer them diamond pensions, so golden their gargantuan greed would finally kick in.

According to Wikipedia, between Congress and the Senate our annual cost of their salaries, pensions, and all other self-created benefits runs into $12.2 billion each year.

The bribes paid by the lobbyists are estimated to equal their official remunerations at the very least.

If we somehow could reason with our politicians and get them jointly to accept $20 billion a year as their pension, they just might listen to us if we make the cash payable the way they like it.

As they hopefully rapidly die off, the country ultimately will be rid of this persistent pestilence.

To help our mission succeed, we could give them a list of the countries where the Mexican crime lords park their money.

We would tell them with our tears running how much we admire them, love them.

We would remind them that they will become historical icons, celebrated as patriots, who sacrificed themselves for the good of their beloved country and already have parks and official buildings named after them.

Privately, we would think, *in the country you robbed for so long.*

We have to constantly keep in mind that due to their lobbyists' bribes and their PAC slush fund, we should avoid that ugly word *cash* and instead use words like *honestly earned* and *deserved pensions.*

These pensions offered with the greatest respect by a grateful people who secretly love them for their unselfish service to a beloved country.

We would also tempt them by offering a celebration of their departure with a patriotic bang-up ceremony, complete with marching bands, the national anthem, and cannons going off as they hand over the keys to the Capitol.

This celebration would be an official recognition for having served our country so well, so unselfishly, always sacrificing their personal interests.

Chapter 6

What breaks in a moment may take years to mend.

Swedish proverb

The purpose of the DIRECT DEMOCRACY system was to provide instant communication between every individual U.S. citizen and their Internet governing center. The voters became the only ones who would make all decisions as to the future course of their country. With the State Department, the Pentagon, and the Federal Reserve gone, a rejuvenated U.S. Treasury along with the other major departments were left intact to implement the decisions made by the voters through the new DIRECT DEMOCRACY system.

One of many positive reasons an exclusive Internet form of government was accepted by the Americans oddly had to do with the fact that many of them, contrary to general belief, are still true introverts. This gives them plenty of time to think, and their quiet reasoning almost always helps them make the right decisions.

It also helped that so many people still considered themselves to be Christian; they learned early in life, from their parents and their church, to show morality in their thoughts and ethics by their deeds.

In addition, when they hear new ideas, they exhibit an innate courtesy, listening carefully. They are known to think on their feet. They also show a flexible quality: Traditional opinions are mutable if intellectual brilliance offers alternatives.

The recent U.S. adoption of *flexicurity* with regard to the choice of location to perform their work is a prime example of this exceedingly rare totally self-reliant quality.

If and when conflicting perspectives are introduced, the Americans receive them with equally respected attention, even if the ideas occasionally are presented late in the discussion when most people show a tendency to wrap up in a hurry. The Americans' conclusions are invariably thoughtful and always generous.

To them, daydreaming is a good thing. Considering that many of the smartest are somewhat low key; only on rare occasions, they quietly, almost reluctantly, allow their solid, independent character to express itself.

Chapter 7

Voting is a civic sacrament.

Fr. Theodore Hesburgh
American clergyman

Switching to the DIRECT DEMOCRACY governing system allowed every voter to be connected by way of iPAD, smart phone, and even those ancient laptops. Not surprisingly, the Americans' first motion was to accept completely all current U.S. laws and regulations as bona fide and legal, possibly as a last compliment to the U.S. ideal form of traditional holistic ubiquity.

Then the next step, with great joy and anticipation, focused on the invitation to allow every American to make individual motions to improve these accepted laws and regulations.

As a result, a number of motions soon addressed a quiet, low-key pruning of many laws and rules created by generations of regulation-happy bureaucrats, aberrations which now, at last, every American could debate and, for the first time, judge against the practical standards of common sense.

Everyone was amazed and amused when they learned how many of these ancient standard regulations failed to get the necessary 67 percent approval.

Thus with every American given the right to vote, an opportunity had been created to have all rules and laws of the country improved and changed should there be a need, provided a plurality of 67 percent of the voters agreed that this should be done.

The beauty of the DIRECT DEMOCRACY system was that suddenly the course of the government was minutely observed, discussed, and acted upon by a new hegemonic population intensely interested and knowledgeable as to where the entire economy and political direction of the country was heading.

After all, everyone in this practical DIRECT DEMOCRACY was given the means to be personally connected, and indeed everyone had a voice, unlike during the discarded representative democracy, which was locked into a market where votes were offered daily for sale, purchased, and then manipulated by the highest paying lobbyists.

Chapter 8

God gives every bird a worm,
but he doesn't throw it into the nest.

Swedish proverb

Here again is a review to make the U.S Direct Democracy system totally transparent.

In Washington, it was recognized that for decades a vast number of lobbyists had been running the country simply by manipulating the congressional vote and guaranteeing legislative actions favoring the fortune of their elusive financial puppet masters.

Instead of having votes constantly offered for sale, Direct Democracy made it mandatory that each American represented only himself or herself. As a result, miracles began to happen since every vote they cast favored the entire country, not, as in the past, just the lobbyists and their financial manipulators.

Almost immediately, as if acting on some pre-ordained priority, the voters launched a massive search for new tax-reducing initiatives. Quickly they created a new austerity philosophy by examining and drastically trimming many costly items in the national budget. Their decisions were made almost instantly due to the Direct Democracy procedure.

Chapter 9

If you're going to walk on thin ice,
You might as well dance.

Inuit (Eskimo) proverb

One of the most admired and respected motions with regard to the reduction of the national budget came from Inuit (commonly known as Eskimos) in Alaska, a tribe with its own practical yet pleasurable culture. It was, for instance, not unusual for Inuits to take off a few days, sometimes as long as a week, in the middle of the winter to go out ice skating with the whole family when their lakes were perfectly frozen.

Since all of them are located north of the Polar Circle with its harsh climate, the Inuits treat their rare visitors with exceptional hospitality. It was not unusual when the temperature dropped drastically below zero for the husband to share his wife's bed with a visitor to keep warm.

Occasionally, in the morning, when the husband went out to fetch fresh snow to make coffee, the wife could be seen giving the visitor a high five.

After learning about this new motion on DIRECT DEMOCRACY, the public media noted with self-congratulatory amusement the omnipresence of the new system with its inclusiveness irregardless of where one lives.

The Inuit's brilliant motion referred to the defense cost which for several years had been escalating.

His motion stated: Why not simply focus all of our military forces exclusively on creating a superior high tech defense and let other countries pick up the cost of conquering the world.

He added that we should let our nuclear-armed and powered submarines remain as a thought-provoking backbone of our defense, which would compel any attacking nation to rethink any aggression.

Then he added, "In view of the devastating direction of the Euro economy supporting too many unemployed people, the United States should offer to sell and guarantee defense to any Euro country if attacked. For this service, the United States would charge an insurance premium set at an engaging discount compared to the amount these financially moribund countries now pay to maintain their often outdated military."

After the proposed motion was announced, something totally unexpected began to happen, and like all pleasant surprises, soon the whole world was laughing heartily.

Seven countries in Africa, five in Asia, and three in South America immediately notified the State Department that they were potential, serious customers. At least, that's how their official emails sounded.

These countries claimed that they could find a much better use for money than warehousing outdated, unused weaponry. They expressed infectious enthusiasm for the U.S. nuclear submarines.

After learning this through the media, the Inuit expressed a vigorous and—do we dare—disarming surprise and added: Why not? Since submarines could travel all over the world, they most certainly could offer timely retaliatory defense to any country close to an ocean.

Then, having created a market, the Intuit cheerfully calculated that this foreign defense premium income could actually nullify America's entire remaining naval defense budget.

Come to think of it, it would most likely provide an unexpected large surplus to help the general budget, thus ingeniously creating the only defense department in the world, running nuclear submarines and a profit.

This refreshing possibility lit up the media for days.

Incidentally, in Florida, something somewhat similar had happened, but here it offered education not defense. The Floridian came up with a somewhat sly name for this brand new dynamic Internet phenomenon: *accidental accreditation.*

It seems that when the Florida Department of Education offered a K-12 Internet curriculum-free program to help their dropouts catch up, they discovered when requiring proof of Florida residence, their most enthusiastic students lived in Georgia, Alabama, and Mississippi.

They also learned that parents in Cuba, Panama, and San Salvador were gladly monitoring a promising dropout rate at Florida's state universities. Hopefully, with a little luck, higher advanced Internet *accreditation* would come next.

Chapter 10

"I know this [gentle justice] system sounds like a curiosity.
But if you visit our prisons and walk our streets,
you will see that this very mild version of
aw enforcement works for us."

Markku Salminen
Former Finnish beat patrolman/homicide detective

To the intellectuals, DIRECT DEMOCRACY had turned into a beauty of a concept, the idea being so simple and powerful, it compelled awe. It quickly but quietly became revered and soon began to inspire voters to submit other unorthodox methods to reduce the U.S. national budget.

One of the first motions turned out to be an eye opener, presenting a radical deviation totally contrary to conventional concepts.

The motions brought to light the fact the exceedingly high cost of running the U.S. prison system.

If this line item could be reduced, it would go a long way toward providing the required funds to put the U.S. budget in the black again.

The motion simply proposed that the very purpose of the penal system had been compromised somewhere back in history and should be updated.

Common sense demanded that all criminals should pay full restitution to their victims for the loss and suffering they caused. An aberration obviously had crept in, at least for white collar criminals, since they found themselves rewarded with a vacation and tennis courts, even if a tad confined. They were also generously fed three meals a day. On special occasions, God forbid, even buffets!

The motion added that in addition to reimbursing their victims, the criminals should be forced to repay the federal or appropriate state government for the costs of their room, board, and medical care.

(On the other hand, if a prisoner were to be found innocent, he or she would be entitled to a comfortable settlement upon release from prison. The compensation for spending many years in prison—not to mention death row—and suddenly be proven innocent would be difficult to calculate, but the motion decided that a set annual amount would be established based on lost livelihood, mental anguish, legal fees, and other factors.)

In order to accomplish this, the need to create new jobs for prisoners was imperative. The motion proposed a federal income tax amnesty to any new company building manufacturing plants inside expanded prison compounds and paying the prisoner/worker prevailing hourly rates.

Another motion suggested that instead of having the judicial system in each case set a time period for a criminal to serve, the court should determine a sum of money to be paid, which incidentally could serve as encouragement for the criminal to work overtime to shorten his incarceration.

When summing up the motion, the DIRECT DEMOCRACY Internet slowed down as everyone paid quiet attention: "Besides, if it came to that, wouldn't you much rather tell folks that you had paid back every nickel you once stole instead of telling them that you had once gone to prison?"

Chapter 11

True beauty in a woman is reflected in her soul.
It is the caring that she lovingly gives,
the passion that she knows.

Audrey Hepburn

Now and then, unexpected motions showed up. One two-part motion created a stir of self-conscious interest all over the United States, because it focused in on a discernable coldness and indifference totally in contrast to the warmth traditionally exhibited by Americans, and likely triggered by the persistent downhill economy.

The motion asked that all Americans be given the opportunity to have their Oxytocin level checked.

As a result of extensive research by Dr. Paul J. Zak, the Oxytocin molecule in the blood explains why some people give freely of themselves and can be trusted with one's life while others are cold-hearted louts; and why women tend to be nicer and more generous than men, and see their Oxytocin count skyrocket when they breastfeed their babies while hugging them.[1]

The motion suggested that since the level of Oxytocin can be increased in people who have built a barrier, a chilly distance between themselves and the rest of humanity, it might be useful for all Americans to find out where their level stands.

However, it was also strongly emphasized that this was not intended to discourage or condemn an anti-social lifestyle, presumably a personal choice, but simply to open everyone's eyes to a possible cause.

The second part of the motion referred to a Harvard University study that would allow all Americans to actually watch as their brains were scanned as dynamic proof that when they talk about themselves, especially if they brag, it triggers the same sensation of intensity in the brain's pleasure center as does food or money.

In view of the colossal cultural contributions the Americans have made toward Western civilization, they should be made aware of and accept being rewarded with this newly discovered feeling of pleasure which their innate modesty would ordinarily automatically downplay.

The motion passed without a single dissenting vote. The first one ever. The Americans were obviously curious.

Chapter 12

"Most Americans have no real understanding
of the operation of the international money lenders.
The accounts of the Federal Reserve System
have never been audited.
It operates outside the control of Congress and
manipulates the credit of the United States."

Barry Goldwater
United States Senator

It is common knowledge that over the years, the U.S. government has engaged in very questionable activities against its citizens by engaging in the process of defrauding some folks of their private savings.

The government first mandated that everybody save some money by placing it into a Social Security account. Since then, to our horror, we learned that the government, with all of its finances directed by the private Federal Reserve Bank, borrowed $2.6 trillion from this private fund owned by individual citizens, telling us that, as a result, the fund will go broke by 2033. [1]

That money has never been paid back to the American people.

Fraud is, incidentally, defined as an activity of taking money from folks under false pretenses.

The disastrous condition of the U.S. Social Security system was highlighted on many Internet blogs. In one blog, it was noted that after the U.S. Social Security System was introduced, instead of investing this entrusted money in safe securities with a decent interest return, the government had chosen to borrow and spend it, thanks to the misguided direction of the Federal Reserve. Unfortunately, Americans, in good faith, had believed that this money would one day cover the cost of their living expenses when they retired or could no longer work.

Instead they were left out in the cold.

Due to the misguided U.S. financial policy, all American citizens were taken on the roughest heartbreak ride ever; the government obviously intended to ruin the golden years of their lives.

Individual Americans, generously labeled naïve, are blinded by highly misguided notions. They do not realize that the historical culture governing them is the result of an overwhelming degree of lawless, enterprising renegades, chased out of Europe for lacking ethics or innate benevolence. Although the most egregious criminals were, thank the Lord, shipped to Australia.

Every foreign visitor must have noticed when traveling across the United States, the local hucksters affably suggesting, "You are not from here, are you?" Then with a big smile while intently watching you, they try to play one of their shell games on you. Some of these attempts are very clever and outrageously comical, and frequent visitors gradually begin to look forward to these encounters.

This particular recurrent play on a newbie being hazed is always done in fun:

He is offered some vittles labeled GREAT LOCAL DELICACY, which turn out to be totally inedible. As his digestive tract sends frantic signals followed by that horrible, hasty expulsion, he ruefully looks around as the locals laugh.

Then we have, quite awhile back, an ambitious Max Hochstim who attempted to open a restaurant in New York. When he bought silverware, he had misgivings and asked the French salesman, "Can I get these with chains?"

Noting the Frenchman's confusion, he added, "To fasten to the table. You don't know the people around here."

In view of this sadly unique, oddly peculiar yet proven American cultural history, this heist of the money the Americans entrusted to their government and saved over a lifetime for their golden years should have been anticipated and should certainly not have come as a surprise.

Indeed, the sad fact of the matter is there was not a noticeable public outcry as to the flagrant disappearance of their personal Social Security savings, which sadly confirmed that Americans had glumly expected this to happen all along.

Incidentally, this was their identical nonchalant reaction to repeated reminders of the rotten state of their for-sale lobbyist democracy.

Many unanswered questions still remained about the disappearance of these trillions in personal savings that Americans entrusted to their government.

For instance, just precisely what role did the private bankers, who own the Federal Reserve, play in the disappearance of these trillions?

Chapter 13

Someday, someone will walk into your life and
Make you realize why it never worked out
With anyone else.

Anonymous

One motion on DIRECT DEMOCRACY ultimately turned out to be the most discussed ever, not only in United States but also across cyberspace.

It was made by Lisa, a girl living in Minnesota in a tradition-bound, mostly Swedish community.

At a summer festival in a few of these communities, residents still put up May poles and generously decorate them with an abundance of wildflowers, delicate newly-leafed birch branches, and intricate garlands. Then around the pole to the quiet amusement of the old timers, the second and third and even fourth generation Swedes do some old-fashioned folk dancing.

The music is played by fiddlers dressed in traditional Swedish folk costumes, obviously delighted as they watch everyone dance around the pole with somewhat exaggerated grace. The dancers laugh as they make each nimble turn required to accentuate these ancient medieval *hambos* and *shottises*.

As a courtesy to tempt visitors to join the festivities, the musicians condescendingly introduce the folk music of other lands such as the Viennese waltz or a South American tango.

One summer, Lisa, a local girl, met an visitor at the festival and, to everyone's surprise, quickly had him swinging along with the intricate hambos and the exuberant shottieses, dutifully stomping both feet at exactly the right moments.

They liked each other's company, and during the following days, they spent hours together.

The following Sunday, she invited him home for dinner to meet her grandmother with whom she lived.

During the dinner, the man suddenly offered: "By the way, I want you to know that I'm married."

The grandmother looked totally bewildered, and obviously Lisa was furious. "But you never told me!"

"That is true, but meeting your grandmother, who is a truly a good person, straightened me out. I had to be upfront and tell you. The truth of the matter is that my marriage has been going downhill for some time. I am on a slippery slope."

The rest of the story you, in fact, could write yourself.

However, something unique happened.

Although their getting together had been so totally fulfilling and pleasurable for Lisa, the man left and they lost contact. Lisa never attempted to track him down and tell him about the baby boy who arrived the following March.

Lisa's parents had questioned her decision, but they both knew that their daughter was emotionally a very strong girl who had shown early streaks of total self-reliance.

She simply told her parents that if the boy turned out to be as intellectually bright and good-looking as his father, she would be happy.

Her parents finally shrugged, looked at her, and laughed, "So, we have another stubborn Swede on our hands. Why should we be surprised?"

Chapter 14

Men marry women with the hope they will never change.
Women marry men with the hope they will change.
Invariably, they are both disappointed.

Albert Einstein

Now married to another village resident with whom she had several children, Lisa made a motion on DIRECT DEMOCRACY that highlighted a problem recognized in every culture: the lack of formal education of and practical training for youngsters one day facing marriage and parenthood.

As we all know, the current universally-accepted high school diploma assures a passable knowledge of how to handle the challenges of an average life.

A college diploma certifies the ability to handle more sophisticated tasks, but no official proof has been agreed upon by our culture to certify a person's ability to become an emotionally, intellectually mature, and caring mate or a safety-oriented, knowledgeable parent.

At the time, no official obligatory training program existed to prepare youngsters for the most important challenges in their lives. This scandalous situation appeared to be the most incredible of the many ignored thresholds in our culture.

Lisa's motion detailed the total innocence with which she had entered into her very first contact with a man. She asked for the establishment of a compulsory one-year high school course to explore a person's ability to maturely choose and accept a life partner, along with a detailed study on how informed upbringing of children should be planned.

It is easily noted that on weekends, every shopping mall in the United States finds youngster milling around, holding accidentally conceived babies, since baby carriages are expensive, trying to give the appearance of being happy.

The impossible task facing these young, often single parents will be to bring up these babies to be well-adjusted, successful adults, which they themselves might never be because of their handicap at birth.

The marriage and family course would offer (1) a detailed study of public records that show why millions of marriages fail each month in America, and (2) the Internet-available records of what happens to parents and young children when parents prove they are unable to properly care for their kids. The only tentative preventive step taken so far to solve the problem is that some public schools hand out morning-after pills to girls as young as fourteen.

After successfully graduating from this course, a certificate would be awarded, a compulsory document required for anyone to be granted a legal marriage license in that community.

However, since we all know too well our human shortcomings and sudden impulses, there still will be relationships that are not sanctified.

The motion passed unanimously without any debate whatsoever.

Rare.

Chapter 15

It is well that the people of the nation do not understand
our banking and monetary system, for if they did,
I believe there would be a revolution before tomorrow morning.

Henry Ford

And thus, along with the daily official routine motions, others sponsored by voters on their own personal missions—a few of them simple without fuss or details—showed up, but all were considered politely and treated respectfully.

In time, the DIRECT DEMOCRACY crowd got together spontaneously on Sunday mornings in an informal Net/chat, referred to as THE CHAT where the week's motions, both passed and rejected, were tasted and digested.

As interest intensified in every country of the world to upgrade to a DIRECT DEMOCRACY form of government, on these Sunday mornings, questions from other countries began to appear.

One question often asked was where do these new ideas come from?

One answer offered that the reason why these motions appeared new is that they come from ordinary folks in the outback of the United States where they still have common sense. DIRECT DEMOCRACY had suddenly provided the pulpit for ordinary folks to bring common sense earned through their life's experiences to the dynamics of governance.

—◆—

Not all comments showing up on Sunday mornings were worthy of recognition or praise.

Everyone laughed when someone in Iceland, claiming to be smart but uneducated, professed that DIRECT DEMOCRACY up to the present was all about wishing, not yet based on hard reality, and therefore seemed dreamy. In truth, it was a lot of *kerfuffle*.

It was immediately noted that somebody claiming to be uneducated had offered an amusing choice of words.

Contributions from Iceland were always received with interest. One opinion from Reykjavik had offered that if you check history, all representative democracies like the one that destroyed the United States end up with dishonesty, deception, and disaster due to the factor of implied trust.

Then it quoted a well-known zoologist, who maintained that even dim-witted dinosaurs in their group endeavors, had practiced representative democracy on a limited basis, and look what happened to them. Everyone laughed.

That remark from the zoologist was, for some curious reason, widely quoted. Seems everybody wanted to know more about the political structure of the dinosaurs whose gas emission is already being studied as it might have changed the climate.

THE CHAT revealed that folks from Iceland, all kidding aside, one-upped the rest of the world in 2008 when they made their government resign, nationalized the banks, and refused to pay the debt created by Great Britain and Holland, due to their bad financial politics (sound familiar?), and created a public assembly to rewrite their constitution. [1]

Three years later, in 2011, Icelandic bankers were arrested, putting the Central Bank of Iceland under investigation, among others. Two bankers have been sentenced to four-and-a-half years in prison: John Thorsteinn Johnsson and Ragnar Gudjonsson.[2]

And the Icelandic people did it without firing a shot.

Peacefully.

Gandhi would have been proud.

—◈—

Totally secure in their new DIRECT DEMOCRACY, the Americans often deplored on THE CHAT the past spectacle of the U.S. representative-controlled democracy run by one war-focused president after another along with a lobbyist-purchased house and senate.

One positive subject discussed repeatedly was the emergence of the dynamic Khan Academy backed by Bill Gates and Google with its free online educational videos originating in the United States and lately moving into classrooms around the world.

Because of the universal nature of science, physics, and mathematics, individuals everywhere can benefit equally from this free service by way of the Internet.

On THE CHAT, it was anticipated immediately that the Direct Democracy system with its universally-useable quality would also some day be equally accepted globally.

One subject made everyone laugh in bewildered wonderment. That subject was how a population consisting of obviously paralyzed U.S. *muppets* had allowed a system, owned by private bankers, to guide the United States into financial disaster, ending in bankruptcy with each U.S. household responsible for $247,000 of the national debt.

Then, in addition, these same gullible *muppets* had submitted themselves into paying income taxes, although there is no law found on the books that would force them to part with their money.

Just plain incredible.

Chapter 16

For so work the honey-bees,
Creatures that by a rule in nature
Teach the act of order to a peopled kingdom.

William Shakespeare

One opinion often expressed on THE CHAT was that the United States obviously did not realize that it had turned itself into a police state by sending delinquent taxpayers to jail based on a fraudulent law. That is the same classical inhumane police state procedure frequented throughout the darkest chapters of human history.

A U.S. citizen from Tibet, new on THE CHAT, told how he was absolutely fascinated when he first watched the spectacle that the United States went through to elect a president.

He commented that it unfortunately looked like blind people were wondering if they could find somebody less blind, but no one was really that sure.

He was also convinced that since all American grade school kids learn about the European kings and their endless wars, they obviously can't wait to grow up, get elected president, and then go to war.

He had brought to the United States his skills as a beekeeper, and in view of the American presidential election, he offered some startling and pertinent tidbits.

He pointed out that none of our Lord's creatures had reached the superior level of organization as that of the honeybees.

Most certainly not the humans.

He wanted Americans in their past election frenzy to realize that the honeybee queen, despite her royal title, does not make a single decision for the hive.

The bees make darn sure that the queen stays put in her fancy honey house and is restrained from offering any opinion whatsoever.

In contrast to the former lobbyist-controlled representative democracy in the United States, the honeybees had developed an advanced direct democracy system for their collective decision-making, which is made through an infinitely sophisticated touch system in some aspect superior to the Internet.

Every single bee is expected, in fact urged, to communicate through this infinite advanced touch system and to offer helpful opinions transmitted to every other bee in the hive.

Studying them reveals their startling level of experimentation and ingenuity.

Since the bees constantly outgrow their hives, they must be on permanent lookout for improved quarters. It is therefore imperative that every bee participates in making necessary decisions.

It had the ring of truth when an entomologist once described New England town meetings as the closest human groupings to honeybee swarms.

The entomologists incidentally refer to this phenomenon as *swarm intelligence.*

Should they ever list *swarm intelligence* in Merriam-Webster, you will find Direct Democracy as its first synonym.

Having been brought up in Tibet, the legendary land found on top of fountains of wisdom, the beekeeper ended with a final gem. "A bee raised on pollen becomes an adult made of flowers."

A thing of beauty.

Chapter 17

"I believe that the banking institutions are more dangerous
to our liberties than standing armies.
The issuing power (of money) should be taken away
from the banks and restored to the people
to whom it properly belongs."

Thomas Jefferson
Third United States President

Among the most noted motions that passed initially was the one to abolish the Federal Reserve Bank immediately.

Another proposed that the finance ministers from Finland, Sweden, Norway, Denmark, and Switzerland be asked to form a committee to determine how the Federal Reserve Bank had so skillfully managed to get the United States into bankruptcy; where all the money had gone; and what part of that dalliance money did the United States pay to the private owners of the Federal Reserve?

One other major motion created much interest. It demanded the licenses of all the media empires be invalidated, citing criminal co-conspiracy for defrauding the American public of the truth about the illegal income tax amendment. Also, for the conspiracy within the media to neglect to monitor, acknowledge, and publish the growing number of successful jury trials in which individuals frivolously charged by IRS lacking legal standing with income tax evasion or attempting to defraud the government were exonerated.

The private nature of the Federal Reserve, responsible for the downward spiral of the United States, was clearly a conflict of interest and should have been the object of Pulitzer Prize-winning investigative journalists, but it was either covered up or just fell through the cracks of mundane day-to-day reporting.

Their licenses were auctioned off to non-media-associated entities.

Chapter 18

We must begin to think like a river,
If we are to leave a legacy of beauty
And life for future generations.

David Brower

The memory of the details of this co-conspired disgrace, which perpetrated human history's greatest heist, orchestrated by the private owners of the Federal Reserve Bank, will live forever.

The anthropologists assure us that our crusty old planet will somehow manage to survive our attempts to destroy it for another fifteen million years.

Every single day of those fifteen million years, this unfathomable, incredible tale of deceit, fraud, and theft of trillions of dollars perpetrated against the people of the United States, the wealthiest nation on Earth, by a small group of bankers will live on with pensive generations demanding to hear what, to them, will sound like the fairy tale of all fairy tales.

To give the tale a balanced air and forestall nightmares, all youngsters most likely would be told that childish gullibility is actually sort of sweet as found by these dewy-eyed Americans.

THE END – OR IS IT THE BEGINNING?

End Notes

Introduction

1. "How Some States Did Not Legally Ratify the 16th Amendment." www. givemeliberty.org of We the People organization.

Chapter 1

1. www.wikipedia.com – Appenzell, Switzerland

2. "Proposed 415-unit housing development to be marketed to Chinese businesspeople." Milan News-Leader, April 11 2012.

3. www.givemeliberty.com

4. YouTube: The Income Tax: WWII Disney Propaganda, "The Spirit of '43," funded and approved by the United States Department of the Treasury. Even President Roosevelt had a say in approving Donald Duck as the main character. In the movie, those who do not wish to pay taxes or don't pay them were depicted as friends of Hitler and enemies of liberty and democracy.

5. Kidd, Devvy. "Make IRS Check Payable to Stockholders of Private FED." April 15, 2005. www.wnd.com.

6. Greenstein, Tracy. "The Fed's $16 Trillion Bailouts Under-reported." September 20, 2011. This article in Forbes magazine (www.forbes.com) states that audit of the Federal Reserve by the Government Accounting Office (GAO) 2008 was the first audit since the FED was founded in 1913. Findings in the GAO audit verified that over $16 trillion were allocated to companies and banks internationally during and after the fiscal crisis of 2008.

7. Matthews, Merrill. "What Happened to the $2.6 Trillion Social Security Trust Fund?" July 13, 2011. Forbes Magazine online at www.forbes.com.

8. YouTube, Senator Sanders Goes off on Bernanke, March 3, 2009, as seen on C-Span 3.

Chapter 2

1.   The "duck hunt" in 1910 included Paul Warburg, Senator Nelson Aldrich (RI), Frank Vanderlip, president, national City Bank, Harry P. Davison, a J. P. Morgan partner, Benjamin Strong, vice-president, Banker's Trust Co., A. Piatt Andrew, former secretary of the National Monetary Commission and current assistant secretary of the Treasury. www.minneapolisfed.org

2.   Griffin, G. Edward. *The Creature from Jekyll Island.*

3.   Founding cartel of Federal Reserve: www.john-f-kennedy.net/thefederalreserve.htm.

4.   Federal Reserve tax-free trillion-dollar annual profits, www.john-f-kennedy.net/thefederalreserve.htm.

5.   Recent Federal Reserve Board of Governors – www.rense.com.

6.   Whitehouse, Michael A. "Paul Warburg's Crusade to Establish a Central Bank in the United States." May 1, 1989. www.minneapolisfed.org.

7.   "Rothschilds and Rockefellers – Trillionaires of the World." December 3, 2007. www.rense.com.

8.   "What Can We Learn from Lehman?" September 15, 2008. www.gettingrichertoday.com.

9.   "A Dollar's Worth in 1913 Costs $23.52 Today." www.minneapolisfed.org. "According to the Federal Reserve, the U. S. dollar has been devalued by 2.352% since the Federal Reserve started in 1913."

10. "Lincoln's Private War: The Trail of Blood." www.servelec.net/lincoln.htm.

11. Fitzpatrick, John Clement, editor. *The Autobiography of Martin Van Buren.* The American Historical Association for the Year 1918. Vol. II (1920).

12. "US Presidents Murdered by the Rothschild Banking Cartel." July 12, 2009. www.rense.com.

13. "America's Forgotten War Against the Central Banks." www.marketoracle.co.uk.

14. http://en.wikiquote.org/wiki/Talk: Woodrow Wilson

15. Told to White House correspondent Sara McClendon, 1992.

16. Curran, John P. "JFK's Executive Order 11110 Abolishing the Federal Reserve." www.rense.com.

17. Schmidt, Robert. "Ron Paul's Fort Knox Fever." June 16, 2011. Bloomberg *Businessweek* magazine. According to this article, Ron Paul, presidential candidate, believes there is no gold in Fort Knox, so he's requesting an independent count of 5,000-plus tons of gold bullion in the Kentucky vault, as well as smaller amounts in Denver, West Point, and New York City. Paul also wants a lab to test the gold bars to be sure they're as pure as the U.S. Treasury says they are.

18. Watson Steve. "House Committee Approves Ron Paul's Audit the Fed Bill." June 28, 2012. www.infowars.com.

19. www.truthattack.org –website of Thomas W. Cryer, Esq.

20. www.irs.gov.

Chapter 8

1.   Unruh. Robert. "IRS loses challenge to prove tax liability." July 26, 2007. www.worldnetdaily.com.

2.   Johnston, David Cay. "Jury Acquits Pilot Who Questioned Liability for Income Tax." *The New York Times*. August 12, 2003.

3.   Vernice Kuglin case. "Winning the 'Unwinnable' Tax Case. www.bernhoftlaw.com.

4.   "Former IRS CID Special Agent Joseph Bannister Acquitted of Tax Fraud & Conspiracy." June 24, 2005. www.givemeliberty.org.

5.   Joseph Bannister case. www.worldnetdaily. March 2004.

6.   Thomas, Ken. January 27, 2012. "Thousands of federal workers owe back taxes." AP. According to this article, from the IRS itself, 279,000 federal employees and retirees owed $3.4 billion as of September 30, 2010; 467 employees of the U.S. House of Representatives owed $8.5 million; U.S. Senate employees owed $2.13 million; and 36 in the president's executive office owed over $833,970.

Chapter 10

1.   Zak, P.J., Stanton, A.A., Ahmadi, A. 2007 "Oxytocin increases generosity in humans. PLoS ONE 2(11).

Chapter 15

1.   "How to Start a Revolution – Learn from Iceland." www.wordpress.com.

2.   "More Icelandic bankers arrested." January 20, 2011. www.icenews.is.

OUTRAGEOUS TAX FACTS

The U.S. tax code is 3.8 million words long. The entire collection of William Shakespeare's works would be about 900,000 words long.

U.S. taxpayers spend more than 7.6 billion hours complying with federal tax requirements.

Seventy-five years ago, the instructions for Form 1040 were two pages long. Today, they are 189 pages long.

There have been 4,428 changes to the tax code in the past ten years.

The IRS currently has 1,999 different publications, forms, and instruction sheets that can be downloaded from the IRS website.

The IRS spends $2.45 for every $100 that it collects.

The United States is the only nation on Earth that tries to tax citizens on what they earn in foreign countries.

The 400 highest-earning Americans pay an average federal income tax rate of just 18 percent.

The top 20 percent of all income earners in the U.S. pay approximately 86 percent of all federal income taxes.

The U.S. has the highest corporate tax rate in the world (35 percent), compared to countries like Ireland at 12.5 percent.

In 1950, corporate taxes accounted for about 30 percent of all federal revenue; in 2012, it will account for less than 7 percent.

Exxon-Mobil paid $15 billion in taxes in 2009 but not a single penny went to the U.S. government.

A total of $18 trillion is being hidden in offshore banks by wealthy Americans to avoid paying taxes.

Source: The Economic Collapse, April 12, 2012

16TH AMENDMENT
RATIFICATION BY STATE

SOURCE: U. S. GOVERNMENT PRINTING OFFICE

1.   Alabama – August 10, 1909

2.   **Kentucky** – February 8, 1909 – approved but then rejected;
Philander Knox considered only the initial approval

3.   South Carolina – February 19, 1910

4.   **Illinois** – March 1, 1910 – **Violation #1*** (The legislature did not
follow protocol that mandates a reading of a constitutional amendment on
three separate days before approving/rejecting it.)

5.   **Mississippi** – March 7, 1910 – **Violation #1** (see Illinois) AND
Violation #2 (Against strict instructions, returned resolution to Knox
uncertified and unsigned and without the official state seal, and no sent no
copy, therefore Knox would not have had any evidence of how the state
legislature voted – a big violation!)

6.   **Oklahoma** – March 10, 1910 – although states are not allowed
to change the wording in a resolution for a constitutional amendment,
Oklahoma changed the wording before approving it, but Philander Knox
accepted the approval without considering their violation of protocol

7.   Maryland – April 8, 1910
8.   Georgia – August 3, 1910
9.   **Texas** – August 16, 1910 – **Violation #1**
10.   **Ohio** – January 19, 1911 – **Violations #1 & #2**

11. Idaho – January 20, 1911

12. Oregon – January 23, 1911

13. Washington – January 26, 1911

14. Montana – January 27, 1911

15. **Indiana** – January 30, 1911 – **Violation #1**

16. **California** – January 31, 1911 – **Violation #2**

17. **Nevada** – January 31, 1911 – **Violation #1**

18. South Dakota – February 1, 1911

19. Nebraska – February 9, 1911

20. North Carolina – February 11, 1911 – Violation #1

21. Colorado – February 15, 1911 – Violation #1

22. North Dakota – February 17, 1911

23. Michigan – February 23, 1911

24. Iowa – February 24, 1911

25. Kansas – March 21, 1911

26. Missouri – March 16, 1911

27. Maine – March 31, 1911

28. **Tennessee** – April 7, 1911 – Illegal action invalidating approval

29. **Arkansas** – April 22, 1911 – Violations #1 and #2

30. Wisconsin – May 16, 1911

31. New York – July 12, 1911

32. Arizona – April 3, 1912

33. **Minnesota** – June 11, 1912 – Violations #1 and #2

34. **Louisiana** – June 28, 1912 – violated state constitutional protocol – disqualified

35. **West Virginia** – January 31, 1913 – Violation #1

36. Delaware – February 3, 1913

According to the U. S. Government Printing Office, ratification was required by 36 states, and without considering the violations noted after each state, ratification was accomplished on February 3, 1913.

*However, Bill Benson in his breakthrough book, *The Law That Never Was*, researched each state thoroughly (in person) and found the above violations (in bold-face), knocking the number of actual states that ratified the 16th Amendment to only 20.

After the 36th state ratified the 16th Amendment (according to Philander Knox) – the following states voted for ratification:

37. New Mexico – February 3, 1913 – Violation #1
38. Wyoming – February 3, 1913
39. New Jersey – February 4, 1913
40. Vermont – February 19, 1913
41. Massachusetts – March 4, 1913
42. New Hampshire – March 7, 1913

The following states never ratified the 16th Amendment:

43. Connecticut
44. Rhode Island
45. Utah
46. Virginia

The following states never considered the resolution:

47. Florida
48. Pennsylvania

HOW TO AMEND THE CONSTITUTION

IN A NUTSHELL

There are two ways to amend the United States Constitution.

Under Article V of the United States Constitution, approval of two-thirds (34 of 50) of the state legislatures is required to apply for a constitutional convention to propose amendments, but Congress actually has the power to call a convention.

So Congress calls for a constitutional convention, but to allay any fears that such a convention might radically alter—or even replace—the Constitution, three-fourths of the states (38 of 50) must ratify any amendments passed by the convention.

Twenty-seven (27) amendments have already been adopted this way. In 1789, the first United States Congress considered 12 amendments, and 11 of those were submitted to the state legislatures for ratification. By December 1791, 10 of those amendments had been ratified and adopted. They became known as the Bill of Rights.

The second way to amend the Constitution has never been done.

This way would allow two-thirds (38 of 50) state legislatures to call for a constitutional convention.

The reason this way has never been used is because Congress likely would not advance any amendments that curtailed its powers. Congress probably would find technical flaws with the states' applications for a convention or would bury them in committee.

Dear Karen,

Thank goodness, I can still email you. I never quite got the hang of tweeting, texting, and all the later technological tricks that you and the youngsters before you have used.

I'm writing this note at the very end of the book, because my very strict editor wouldn't let me write an epilogue. She thought I was being too repetitious, but I did want to mention a few other items that Americans, through DIRECT DEMOCRACY, managed to vote into law.

1. The immediate termination of all financial support to other countries (with no exceptions). Of course, in the event of horrific natural disasters, the Americans, as others around the world, would make generous contributions.

2. Free medical care for every American citizen, regardless of age, just as the Swedes provide their citizenry.

3. Totally free advanced education at all state universities, again as is done in Sweden.

4. Conversion of all education at the primary level from the classroom to the Internet instruction, with the hope that it will more effectively improve the American standard of education, which was lagging behind in every measurable category for far too long.

Karen, I hope you will love my little book. It would have been bigger, but my editor kept reminding me that a book about mice and cheese was only 98 pages long, and it sold millions. If this one does the same, I suppose I'll have to give her a bonus.

I'm happy that DIRECT DEMOCRACY became a reality before you were born. Life here now is more like I remembered it when I first arrived in America.

Love,
Grandpa

www.ingramcontent.com/pod-product-compliance
Lightning Source LLC
Chambersburg PA
CBHW021838020426
42334CB00014B/688